Walter Chandoha's Book of Puppies and Dogs

By the same author

Walter Chandoha's Book of Kittens and Cats

Walter Chandoha's Book of Puppies and Dogs

BONANZA BOOKS · NEW YORK

Walter Chandoha's Book of Puppies and Dogs

Introduction

Dogs come in all shapes, sizes, and colors. They are small—so small that you could fit one in your pocket. And they are big—big enough to pull a cart. Some are short and long, some are tall and thin. Some are smooth, some are wiry, and some are hairy. Some are even hairless.

A dog can be a purebred with a pedigree that can be traced back a score or more generations. Or a dog can be a mixed breed—a mutt—of dubious ancestry, born of parents of uncertain heritage.

Mutt, mongrel, mixed breed—call it what you will—it's still a dog, and it will love you no less than the purest of purebreds.

A mutt is a hybrid, a cross between two unlike canines, which results in offspring that may be similar to the male, similar to the female, or unlike either. I think the uncertainty of how a mutt will ultimately look when fully grown makes it all the more interesting.

In horticulture, hybrids of various types are not only more desirable than pure strains, but are practically the only types available. Hybrid roses are a good example. Hybrid corn is another. There is hardly a farmer today who plants anything but hybrid corn.

Yet, in the dog world—the elite dog world of dog shows, kennel clubs, field trials, publications, and dog food merchants—the hybrid dog is looked down upon and largely ignored.

I like mutts and I like purebreds too. In our house we have one of each. Our Bouvier des Flandres, a purebred with a pedigree a mile long, comes from the Dewall kennel. Our mutt—Max—is an unknown variety, but he is as devoted and as affectionate as Kittydog, the Bouvier.

Kittydog was acquired after many years of having nothing but pet cats for our children. She was so named because of the cats. When the cats are called for their meals, they respond to "Kitty, kitty, kitty," repeated rapidly. When they hear this call they come running. And so did the Bouvier pup. Since she was responding to "Kitty" so readily, we decided to add DOG to KITTY and make KITTYDOG her official name.

Max was so named because I like the name Max. It's a good, short, sharp masculine name that conforms with my idea of what a male name should be. When I hear what some boys and men are called nowadays I wonder what has happened to the good old names like Hank, Sam, Charlie, Frank, Al, Steve, Tom, and Max.

The names people give dogs today are almost as unbelievable as the names they give to boys and girls. Even a good honest dog name like Fido can be corrupted. It's still pronounced Fi'do, but to add an aura of something or other, the spelling is changed to "Phydeau."

Hardly anyone calls his dog Rex or King or Queenie or Trixie anymore. Or even Chubby. When I was a child we had a Chubby in our family. And, as I recall, there were half a dozen other Chubbies in the neighborhood. And there were a lot of Tootsies too.

Whatever names the dogs of today are stuck with, fortunately for me they almost all respond to their names when called. This makes dog photography somewhat easier than cat photography, as cats rarely respond to their names. But even though dogs do answer to their names, there are other problems in dog photography. The owners of the dogs, for one. Many of them are not too patient.

My wife, Maria, who very ably assists me when I take

my dog pictures, can do wonders in getting a dog to cooperate in front of the camera. We both have a good deal of patience and know that sooner or later we can get a dog to do anything within reason that is required. All it takes is kindness and time.

Unfortunately, some dog owners are very impatient —especially if they pride themselves at being great dog trainers. Say we need a simple shot, perhaps a dog sitting in a chair with its head and paws resting on the arm. Now, if a dog is brought into a strange place (our studio) and asked to do this, he may be reluctant to, especially if he is forbidden to get up on the furniture in his own house.

If the dog fails to stay in the desired pose in the chair, at first his owner will beg and cajole. As the dog persists in refusing to cooperate, the owner feels he is losing face, and he proceeds to make his commands louder and harsher. I can usually judge by the owner's voice whether his next step may be physical punishment. So, as diplomatically as I can, I try to persuade him to go for a walk or go to the study over the studio and read some magazines.

With the impatient owner out of the way, Maria and

I can usually get our dog model to cooperate. At some time during a shooting session, even the most obstinate dog will catch on to the idea of what he must do, and he'll do it. Most of the time!

Then there's the dog and owner who are especially fond of each other. One such case concerned a big brindle bulldog. The love he had for his mistress and she for him was a delight to behold. But try to take pictures of a bulldog alone when he wants to sit on the lap of his mistress and be petted—impossible!

I told the owner I was pleased that she and the dog were such great pals, but that we might do better if she were not in the studio. As soon as she left, we were able to make some great pictures of the English bulldog in a short time.

Sometimes it takes hours—even days—before a dog will cooperate. During this "acquaintance" period we do not make a single exposure. At other times when a dog comes to the studio, I will arrange the lights while Maria gets the dog in place and in the desired pose, and we'll start shooting and be through in an hour.

This brings to mind a question that I'm often asked about one or another of my dog photographs: "How long did it take to get that picture?" The answer may be 1/5000 of a second, the time it takes for my strobe to flash.

Actually, most of my pictures are the result of much planning. As in any creative endeavor, the planning takes more time than the execution or the experiencing. Take a movie—you can see the average one in about ninety minutes, yet it took months to shoot and maybe a year or two to plan.

With my dog photographs I first have to think about what I want to put on film—what is the situation, the type of dog, the color of the background; what props, if any, do I need; what will the setting be? Then I have to locate and actually see and handle the dog in his home environment to get an idea of his temperament and personality.

Some dogs, like some people, are neurotic and high-strung, and are not very good camera material. On the other hand, others—both dogs and people—have a happy, outgoing personality that is reflected in a good photograph.

Having checked the dog out, I next build the set with the required background and props. At the appointed time the dog arrives, and—hopefully—we make some interesting photographs.

A good example of a dog's happy personality being reflected in his photographs is that of a silky terrier I met some time ago at a dog show. Outdoor dog shows are much like the circus when it was a tent show. There are numerous tents, and a great many people are walking about in a somewhat festive mood. Dog owners are leading leashed dogs to and from the show-rings. Spectators are seated or standing around the rings watching the action. Old friends gather in small groups and relive other dog shows in other places. Vendors of various dog products are hawking their wares.

At one of these dog shows, I came upon a silky terrier tied to a tent stake, watching all the activity. He was completely at ease and unperturbed by the hubbub around him. As I bent down to pet him, his stump of a tail wagged furiously and his bright eyes said hello. If the dog was this friendly, happy, and alert in all the confusion of the dog show, I figured he'd be even more so in the quiet of my studio. So I waited for his owner to appear. She was a most attractive young lady.

I identified myself and asked if we might arrange a

mutually convenient time for her to come to my studio with the dog for a photographic session. As I handed her my card, it occurred to me that everything I said sounded like the old come-up-and-see-my-etchings proposition. To allay any suspicion along these lines, I made sure to mention that my wife would probably answer the phone when she called to arrange a shooting date. She called the following week, and the photographs we made of her charming dog were everything I had expected.

Rarely do I ask an owner to bring a dog to my studio to be photographed unless I have a specific assignment, but when I find a model as appealing as that little silky terrier, I make every effort to fit him into my shooting schedule. The pictures that resulted turned out to be very successful.

Some sessions are not so successful. One assignment that comes to mind was a picture we had to make of a dog sitting up and begging. In checking my sources, I found the required breed that would sit up and beg on cue. I went to the dog's home to check out its temperament and appearance. Both were excellent. He was a happy dog, he appeared to be healthy and alert, and—best of all—he begged every time he was tempted with a morsel of food. This, I thought, would be one of those easy assignments where the dog comes into the studio, we start shooting, and the job is completed in a few hours.

I was right about finishing quickly—but we finished without the pictures.

The dog arrived at the studio, happy and eager to work. As soon as my lights were arranged, he was brought onto the set. We tried a few dry-run begging poses, and everything went along smoothly. "Let's start shooting," I said.

The dog was in position, sitting up and begging beautifully. I fired the first flash. When it went off, so did the dog. He literally flew out of the shooting area into the reception room, where he crawled behind a couch and whimpered like a baby. The dog was flash-shy! Nothing we could do would get him back under the lights. We tried dog biscuits, liverwurst, cheese, and even a choice cut of steak. All without success. So, rather than waste any more time, we dismissed the dog and his owner and went back to our files to find another model that would beg on command.

When I checked the next dog, I not only made sure he would beg as required, but to make certain he was not flash-shy, I fired my portable flash a few times. He worked out fine.

Though I've photographed many dogs—easily, thousands—I've been bitten only once. And that time I should have known better. We had a large hound in the studio, and had spent most of the day taking excellent pictures of him. When we were finished, I went out to the drive with the owners to bid them farewell. Since the dog had worked so well before the camera, I felt I should also say thanks and good-bye to him. As I put my hand in the car window to pat his head, there was a snarl and the sound of snapping jaws. Luckily, I was able to withdraw my hand with no more than a couple of fingers gashed and bloodied! Only then did they tell me that the dog was very protective of his home and the car. I had to agree that he was an excellent watchdog!

Another unique experience with one of my dog models occurred at a dog show on Long Island. At shows I frequently run into friends whose dogs I've used at one time or another. Sometimes the dogs remember me—sometimes they don't. This particular afternoon, I was remembered in a most doglike way. As I stood chatting with the dog's owner, I felt an unusual warmth on my leg. To my surprise, I found the dog had used my leg as he would a fire hydrant. My habit of wearing washable slacks to dog shows is not without good reason.

Dog shows are primarily contests among dogs to determine which one is the best of any given breed, the best of a group, and the best dog in the show. The best of breed makes sense, and the best of group could be justified. But to judge one dog the best of show seems asking for the impossible. How can the best Great Dane be judged against the best beagle or the best Chihuahua? It's like saying apple pie is better than steak, or strawberry jam is better than fried chicken. Each is excellent in its own category, and cannot be honestly judged better or worse than the top choice in another group.

In addition to its contest aspect, the dog show is also a social event. Dog-club people gather, and special tents are set up where lavish buffet luncheons are served. Tailgate picnics are numerous. Families bring their children to see most of the 115 breeds approved by the AKC (American Kennel Club), and perhaps to choose a family pet.

The people who go to dog shows are, for the most part, splendidly attired. Unlike me (my dog-show working clothes consist of sneakers, a pair of chinos, and a sport shirt), most of the men are dressed in the latest sportswear. The ladies are even more attractive in shapely shorts, dainty Dacron dresses, or, more recently, form-fitting slacks. The mixture of tastefully flamboyant garb and stylish sportswear seen at dog shows brings to mind the expression, "I wouldn't wear that to a dog show," to indicate that a certain garment is not quite acceptable.

From my observation, just about anything can be worn to a dog show and look right—outlandish hats, gaudy ties, frilly blouses, bulky tweeds, custom-tailored suits, even denim jeans. Actually, the expression should be changed to "That would look great at a dog show."

There are many other expressions and phrases in the language in which some form of the word *dog* is involved. Some of these make sense; others do not, like the one just mentioned.

A comparison that seems to be out of place today is "I worked like a dog"—that is, hard, long, and diligently. Dogs don't work hard; in fact, they scarcely work at all. Except for a few circus performers and sled dogs, even so-called working dogs don't really work *that* hard.

Certainly a field dog looking for birds isn't working; he's having fun. And a guide dog for a blind person is not physically working hard, though he may be under considerable strain. A sheep dog works a bit, but not to exhaustion. Thus, when anyone says he's been working like a dog, maybe he's telling the truth and has in fact been laboring like the majority of family pet dogs, who are spoiled and pampered.

And they are also groomed. In any large city, dog beauty parlors are commonplace. Here the dogs are shampooed, plucked, coiffed, clipped, and manicured. Combine the beauty parlors with the grooming services of kennels and veterinarians, and you have a lot of clean dogs. So why the expression, "You dirty dog!"?

Being "hounded" is a valid dog-type expression if it

means to be constantly and incessantly nagged or chased. It stems from the ability of a hound to trail and pursue a quarry.

"Bird-dogging" is another valid expression. I once heard a suspicious salesman ask a would-be customer, "Who are you bird-dogging for?" The salesman suspected the customer didn't really want to buy but was extracting information for a third party.

Women are inclined to call other women "bitches" or "bitchy" when they mean a woman is petty, cranky, jealous, and generally cantankerous. Yet most bitches I know—female dogs, that is—have a generous, friendly, pleasing personality.

Why does a cowboy call his young motherless calves "dogies," and why do we call a frankfurter a "hot dog"? Doggerel is the lowest form of poetry, and dog days are the hottest, most uncomfortable days of summer. More than one golfer has had his score ruined by a hole with a dogleg. And if you must dog-ear a page of this book, do it now on this page—but next time please use a bookmark.

If you should hear a couple of soldiers talking about a dog robber, don't think one of them is in the business of stealing dogs—they're talking about a soldier-servant to a high-ranking officer. (The military gives the servant term more dignity by calling a dog robber an orderly.) Dog tags are not worn by dogs—they are the metal identification tags worn by people in military service. In the army we called soldiers "dogfaces."

"Putting on the dog" and being "doggy" are expressions used to belittle someone's pretentious airs or attempts at being stylish.

And so it goes. The dog is well represented by words and expressions in the English language, but most of these have an unsavory or negative connotation. Luckily, among writers the dog has had many admirers who show him in a favorable and positive way.

E. B. White, G. B. Stern, Rudyard Kipling, Hugh Walpole, Robert Louis Stevenson, Don Marquis, D. H. Lawrence, Alexander Woollcott—the list is endless—are just a few of those who have written about dogs.

One of the most outstanding dog writers was Jack London. I vividly remember my childhood enthusiasm for his stories. *Call of the Wild* and *White Fang* were my favorites.

Now, with my greater understanding of dogs and my involvement with them through photography, I have even more appreciation for London's stories.

Those of us who love dogs can relate to London's description, in *Call of the Wild,* of how John Thornton's dog Buck showed his affection for his master by taking John's hand in his mouth and closing "so fiercely that the flesh bore the impress of his teeth for some time after." Thornton's other dogs would show their affection in other ways. One would shove his nose under John's hand and nudge until he was petted. Another would come and rest his big head on John's knee, for petting and affection.

James Thurber's cartoon drawings of dogs have amused the readers of *The New Yorker* for many years. The sequence of the hound and the hat probably summarized his thinking about the relationship between any man and his dog. It showed a dog happily chewing a lady's hat. When the lady of the house unexpectedly returned home, her husband—to save the dog from punishment—picked up the hat and started chewing on it just as his wife came in the door, while the dog innocently looked on.

The Thurber cartoon sequence reminds me of the numerous occasions when I've disposed of chewed-up shoes and gloves that our dogs had mutilated. The culprit was spared a reprimand, and, together, we actually performed a service by getting rid of some of the excess footwear that seems to litter homes where there are several children.

As good an artist as Thurber was, he is better known for his writings on dogs. His humorous, tongue-in-cheek accounts of dogs he has known—either real or imaginary—are classics. I believe it was Thurber who once said that the dog had got more fun out of man than man out of the dog—because man is the more laughable of the two.

One of the best-known writers on dogs was Albert Payson Terhune. Collies, which were frequently featured in his stories, were his favorite dog subject. On his farm, Sunnybank, he raised prize-winning show collies, and their exploits provided him with an endless source of material for his dog stories.

Lad was one of Terhune's favorite collies and the subject of three of his books. An episode involving Lad that I found especially amusing concerned the time the Terhunes visited an ailing lady friend who seemed to be somewhat of a complainer. As she told the Terhunes of her misery, she punctuated her account with frequent moans and groans. Lad, hearing these sounds, proceeded to howl and whine in accompaniment with the hypochondriac, which pleased her immensely!

This performance of Lad's is similar to the behavior of our Kittydog, who does much the same thing with our daughter Chiara. But with Chiara and Kittydog, it's a deliberate put-on. As Chiara commences to sing, Kittydog will sit beside her, throw back her head, and whine in perfect discord.

Along with writers, artists have been using the dog as a subject for thousands of years. In some archeological digs near Thebes in Greece, among the other things found were various objects bearing the likenesses of dogs; these dated back to 4000

B.C. A couple of thousand years later the Egyptians were making extensive use of the dog in their jewelry, drawings, and sculpture.

Later, some of the great painters in the tradition of the "old masters" used the dog in their works—to name a few: Goya, Rubens, Vandyke, Rembrandt, Botticelli, and Holbein. In most of the works by these painters the dog was an incidental part of the painting. But as insignificant as the dogs were to the overall painting, the renderings give us a good idea, today, of what the dogs of yesterday were really like.

Through the years, the breeds evolve and change imperceptibly—a snout may be elongated as in the collie; body structure may become stockier or more slender. Most of the changes happen so gradually, over a period of many years, that we are unaware a change in a breed is actually taking place. Yet over a span of fifty years to a century, some of the breeds change drastically.

If we compare the standard poodle of today with the poodle that appears in Renoir's "At The Inn of Mother Anthony," painted in 1866, we find little similarity between the two poodles. And the Old English sheepdog in Phillip Reinagle's painting, *ca.* 1800, has not the slightest resemblance to the Old English sheepdog of today. The pug in William Hogarth's "Self Portrait" is somewhat taller than today's standard of that breed. He also seems to be leggier, and his nose is longer.

On the other hand, "King Charles and Blenheim Spaniels" in Sir Edwin Landseer's painting of that name, done over a century ago, are almost identical to those dogs today.

Perhaps, because of his accuracy in depicting canines, Landseer might rightfully be called the dean of dog painters. A great number of his paintings featured the dog as the dominant subject. His almost photographic realism combined with his obvious rapport with dogs makes his studies an invaluable record of the dogs of his era.

The dogs of our era are living in a Golden Age far more glorious and golden than any era of the past. Even the dogs of ancient Egypt who were worshipped as gods did not have it as good as the majority of today's dogs.

Of the twenty-five to thirty million dogs in the United

States today, the vast majority are mutts. Most of these hybrids and a good number of purebreeds are family pets. They are in the house as part of the family—living, eating, playing, and sleeping with their human masters. Years ago, the family pet was fed with table scraps; he rarely saw a veterinarian and was never bathed or groomed by a professional.

Today it's a different story. First of all, the family pet is usually bought rather than gotten free. Pet shops with as many as twenty-five to a hundred pups on display and for sale are commonplace. They do a big business—so big that some of the more enterprising pet-shop chains are selling franchises to inexperienced individuals to open more pet shops in other communities.

Shortly after a pup is acquired he is taken to the vet for various shots. Then his new owner makes the first of many, many trips to the supermarket for puppy food. Then back to the pet shop to buy a collar and leash and maybe a few toys. Before long, the pup must be taken to the vet for worming. The owner continues the endless trips to the supermarket for dog food, to the drugstore for vitamins. Soon it's time to enroll the dog at the training school for obedience lessons. And there are regular visits to the kennel for a shampoo and haircut.

And, of course, there's boarding the dog during vacation or buying a travel carrier to take him along or ship him by plane. And more dog food. Finally sex enters the picture, and it's off to the vet once more for either neutering or locating an appropriate mate.

When puppies arrive, the whole process starts over again—four, five, or six times, depending on the number of pups.

In the pet food area alone the American public spends over a billion dollars—that's *billion*, not million—annually. To this, add several billions for more medical care and related products, beauty care and preparations, and the hundreds of other dog items that are on the market.

What does all this mean to the dog? Well, he couldn't be happier about it. First, the food situation. When he was fed table scraps his diet was unbalanced and inconsistent. Now, the nutritionists at the various dog food companies see to it that commercially prepared dog food is well fortified with all the vitamins and minerals a dog requires.

He's also certainly better off visiting the vet and getting inoculated against distemper and rabies. And he is far happier without the problem of worms that probably plagued his ancestors thirty or forty years ago.

Obedience training could save his life. More than one impetuous dog has been hit by a car as he recklessly ran into the street in pursuit of a cat. The simple commands "stay" or "no" may check the dog and spare him the agony of a crushed body.

And why shouldn't a dog be clipped, coiffed, groomed, and shampooed—if he's that type of dog?

So, all in all, I would say the dog is enjoying his new Golden Age. Couldn't happen to a nicer creature!

Great Dane and Pomeranian

Beagle

English Bulldog

Great Dane

Chihuahua

Chihuahua

Boxer Pup

Great Dane

Great Danes

Silky Terrier

Poodle

Scottish Terriers

Welsh Springer Spaniels

Boston Terriers

German Wirehaired Pointer

Mutt

German Shepherd

47

Bouviers des Flandres

Mutt

Bloodhound

Bloodhound

Bedlingtons

Dachshund

Dalmatian

Irish Setter

Bulldog

Pointer

Poodle

Brittany Spaniel

Australian Terrier

Basset Hound

Poodles

Dachshund

Malinois

Boxer

Scottish Deerhounds

Dachshund

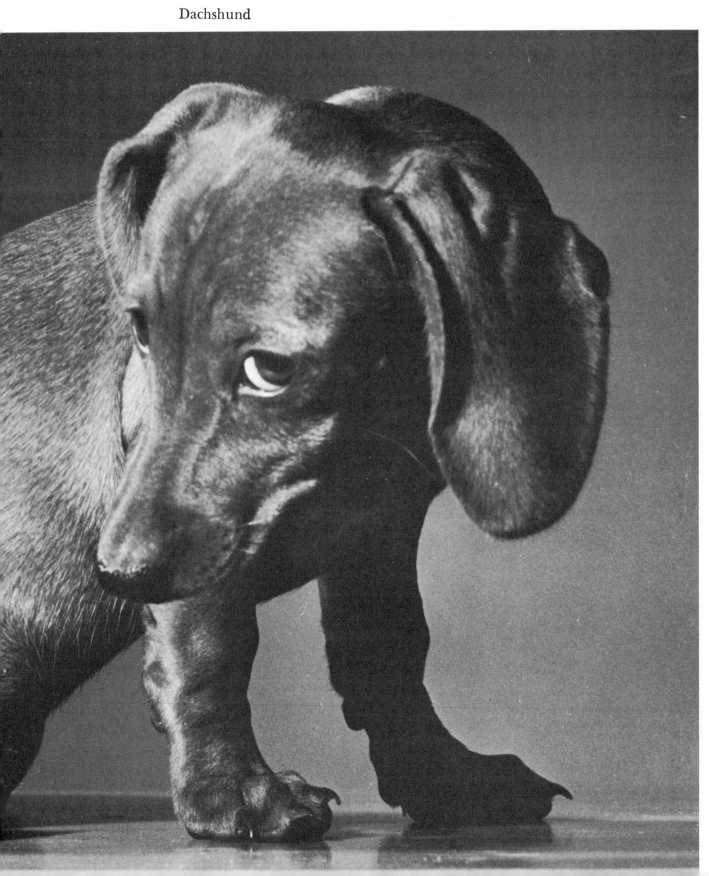

Mutt

Boston Terrier

Beagles

Afghans

Boxer

Mutt

Mutts

Sealyham

Golden Retriever

Basset Hounds

Japanese Spaniels

Mutt

Dalmatian

Springer Spaniel

Veimaraner

Scottish Deerhounds

Bouvier des Flandres

Bouvier des Flandres

Border Collie

Border Colli

Mutt

Maltese

Papillons

German Shepherds

Keeshonden

Cocker Spaniel

Cocker Spaniel

Bouvier des Flandres

Bull Mastiffs

Doberman Pinschers

Beagles

Sealyhams

Saluki

116

Weimaraner

Greyhound

Malamute

Toy Poodles

oodle

Malinois

Mutt

Beagle

English Cocker Spaniel

Pointer

Weimaraner

Pekingese

rish Terrier

Saint Bernards

Miniature Pinscher

Boston Terrier

136

Samoyed

Schipperke

Weimaraners

English Toy Spaniel

Mutt

Bouvier des Flandres

Mutt

Harriers

Norwich Terrier

Pugs

Irish Setter

Irish Setter

Mutt

Golden Retriev

Puli

Mutts

Golden Retriever

Fox Terrier

Bouviers des Flandres

Labrador Retriever

Labrador Retriever

Beagles

German Shorthaired Pointers

Irish Terrier

Beagle

Beagle

English Bulldogs

Scottish Terrier and West Highland White Terrier

Mutt

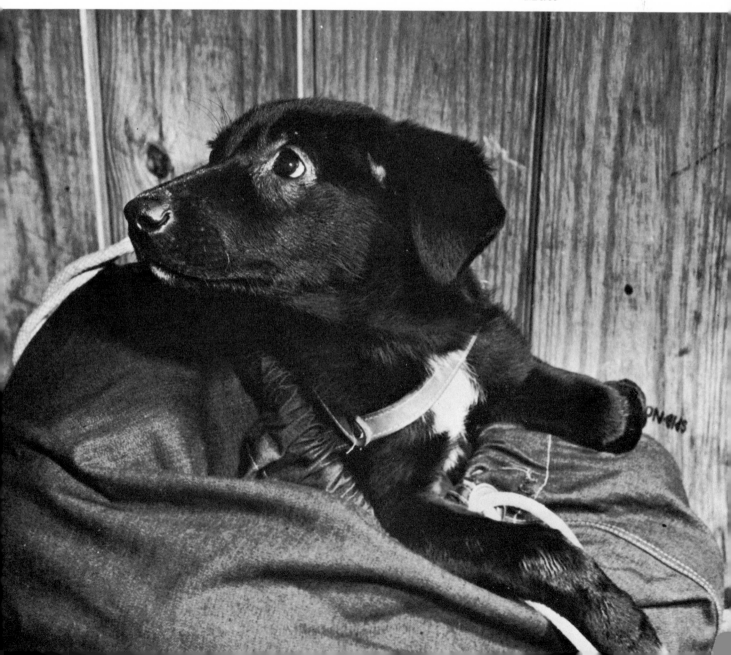

Siberian Husky

Collie

Norwegian Elkhounds

Maltese

Manchester Terrier

Toy Fox Terriers

Great Dane

Mutt

179

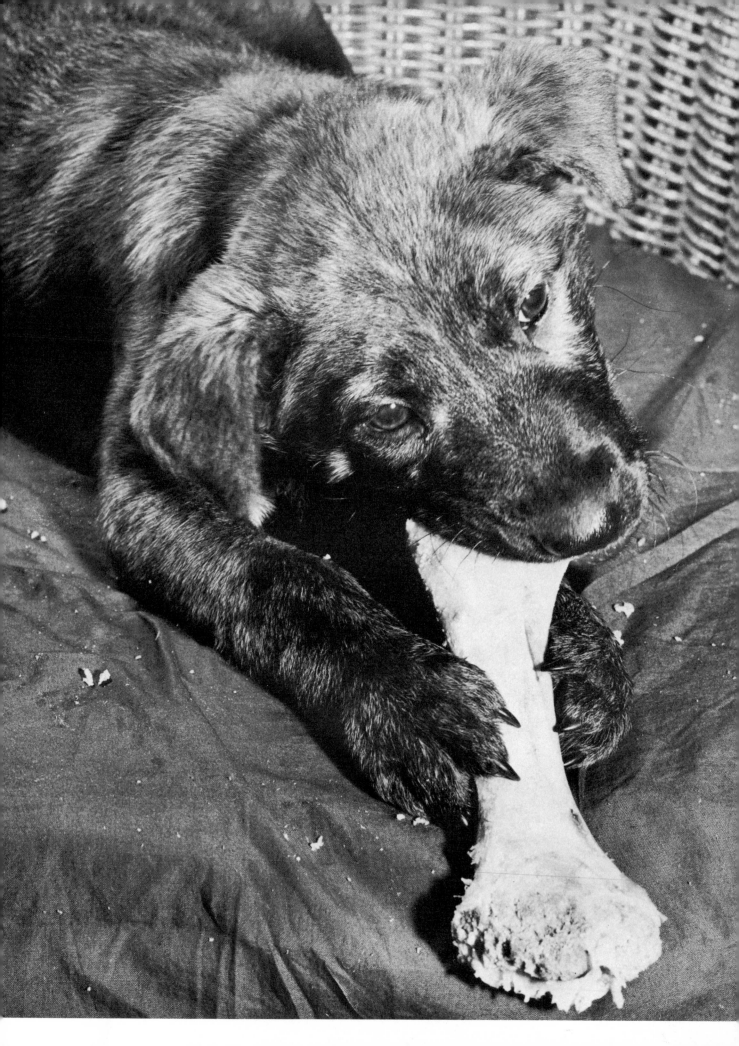

Collie and Shetland Sheepdog

Mutt

Chihuahua

Basenji

Mutt and Beagle

Mutt

Collie

Bouviers des Flandres

Mastiff

Miniature Schnauzer

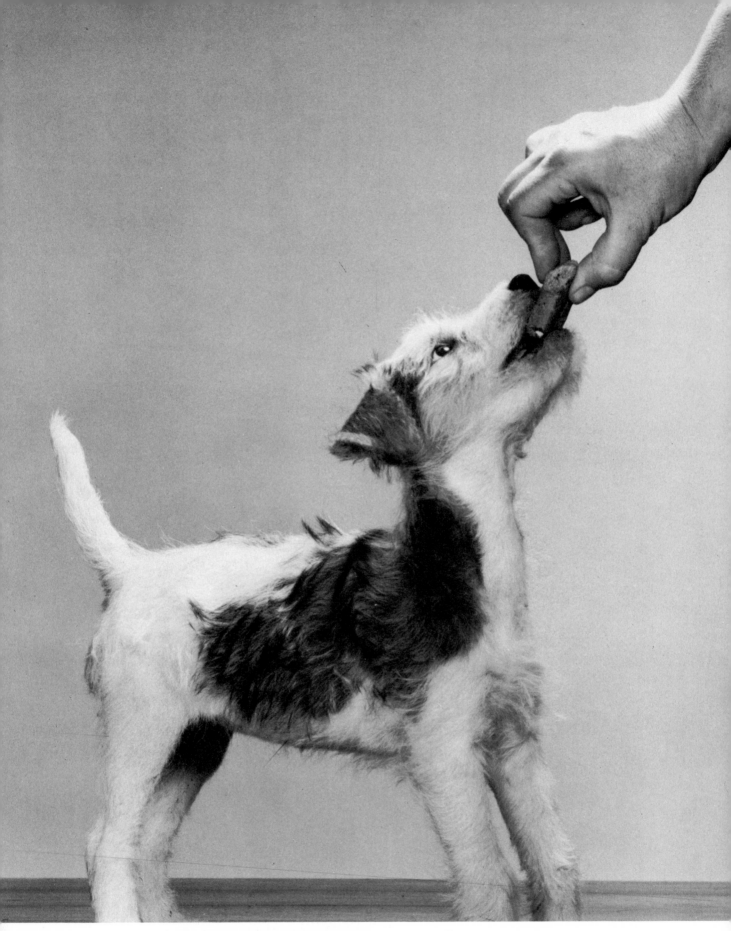

Wirehaired Fox Terrier

Cocker Spaniel

Cocker Spaniel

Irish Setter

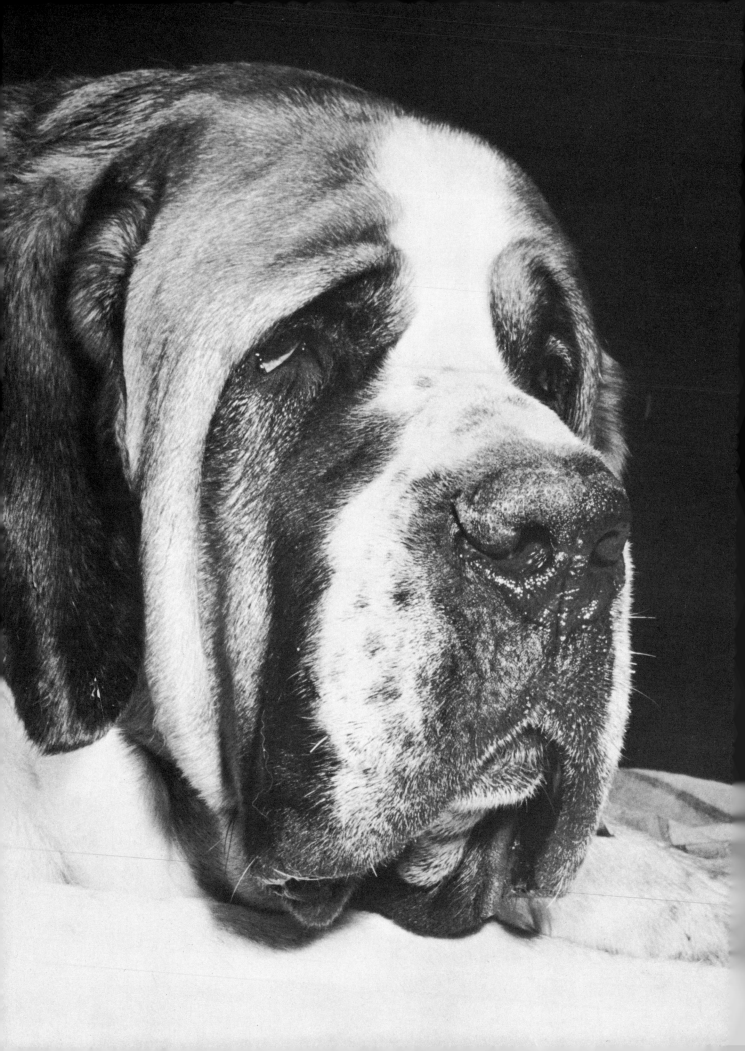

Poodle

St. Bernard

Labrador Retriever

Boston Terrier and Dachshund

Dalmatian

Mutt

Doberman Pinscher

Fox Terrier

Irish Wolfhound

Vizsla

Brussels Griffo

English Sheepdog

Shih Tzus

Mutt

Silky Terrier

Cocker Spaniel

Harrier

Otterhound

Mutt

Dachshund

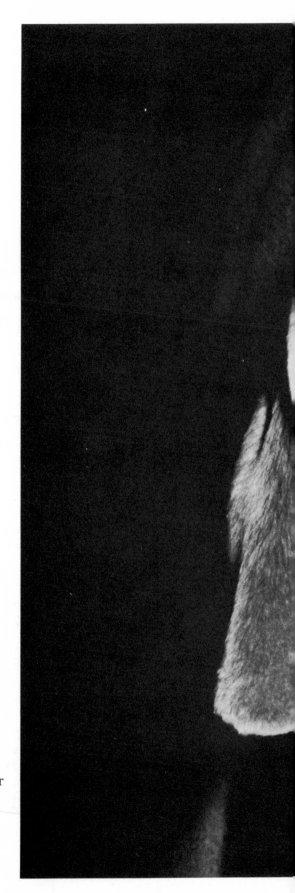

Weimaraner

Affenpinscher

Boxers

226

Yorkshire Terrier

Siberian Huskies

Bedlingtons

Wirehaired Fox Terriers

Boxer

Pomeranian

German Wirehaired Pointer

Weimaraner

Miniature Pinscher

Sealyham

Beagle

Dachshund

Beagle

Pointers

Welsh Terrier

West Highland White Terriers

Irish Terrier

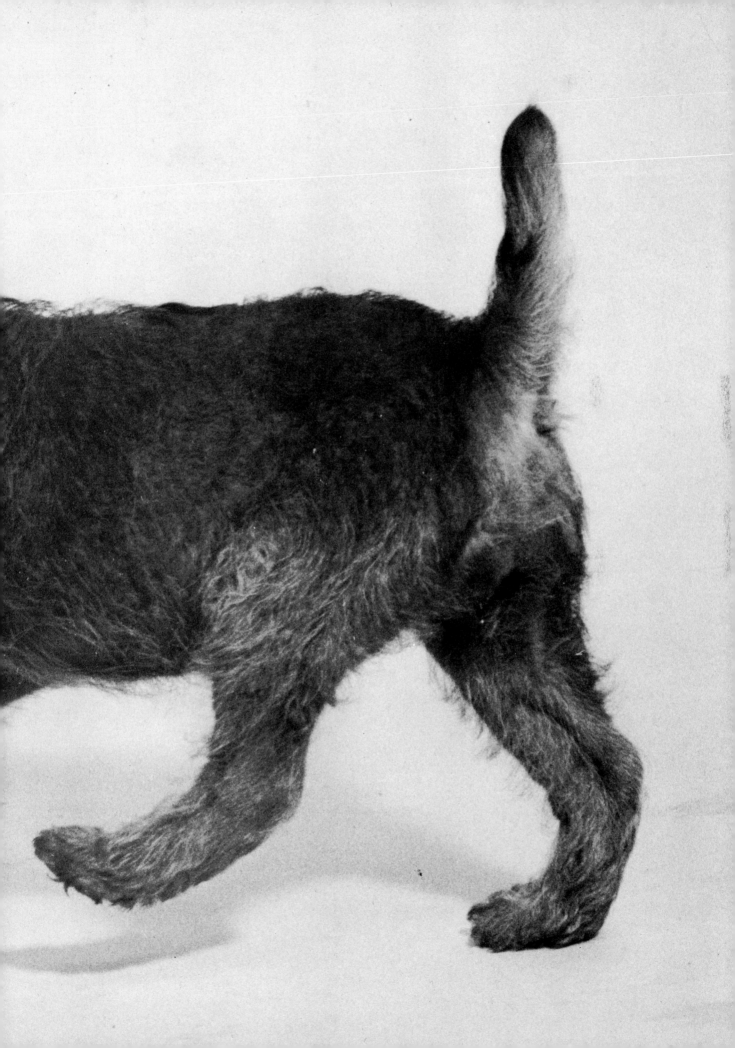

Shetland Sheepdog

English Bulldog

Fox Terrier

English Setters

Welsh Corgi

Chihuahua

Lhasa Apsos

Mutt